Contents

Finding My Way Home

HENRI J.M. NOUWEN

Finding My Way Home

PATHWAYS TO LIFE AND THE SPIRIT

A Crossroad Book
The Crossroad Publishing Company
New York

The Crossroad Publishing Company
481 Eighth Avenue, New York, NY 10001

Printed in the United States of America

Library of Congress Cataloging-in-Publication Data

Nouwen, Henri J. M.
    Finding my way home : pathways to life and the spirit /
Henri J. M. Nouwen.
      p. cm.
    Includes bibliographical references.
    ISBN 0-8245-1888-8
    1. Christian life – Catholic authors.   I. Title.
BX2350.3 .N68 2001
248.4′82 – dc21

                          00-012575

1 2 3 4 5 6 7 8 9 10   06 05 04 03 02 01

To Kathy Christie

Foreword

I recently returned from Toronto after spending six marvelous days with the L'Arche Daybreak community in Richmond Hill, where Henri Nouwen spent the last ten years of his life. It was an inspiring visit!

My journey back to New York, however, was very frustrating; LaGuardia Airport was forbidding planes to depart for New York. As a result, numerous planes were delayed and hundreds of passengers stranded. Fortunately, we were able to get on a flight to Newark, where the air traffic was less congested, but the whole experience was one of frustration. I could have flown to California in the time it took me to "find my way home" that night.

In *Finding My Way Home*, Henri Nouwen writes about "journey" in a very different way:

Our spiritual journey calls us to seek and find this living God of Love in prayer, worship, spiritual reading, spiritual mentoring, compassionate service to the poor, and good friends. Let us claim the truth that we are loved and open our hearts to receive God's overflowing love poured out for us.

It sounds so simple! Our journey, then, is a journey to discover the perfect love that only God can give us.

But how do we remain faithful to this journey? The frustrations of making a spiritual journey are similar to the frustrations I felt at the Toronto airport. What do we do when our spiritual journey runs into roadblocks? When waiting makes us anxious and angry? Nouwen writes, " . . . waiting is a dry desert between where we are and where we want to be." We are encouraged to look at waiting from two perspectives: the waiting *for* God and the waiting *of* God. Most of us think more about the first perspective, but as we grow in our awareness of God waiting and longing for us, we discover the deepest love there is—God's love.

Henri Nouwen is a companion on the journey for me

and for countless people around the world. But for Henri, and for us, Jesus is our principal guide: "We want to look with God's eyes at our experience of brokenness, limitedness, woundedness, and frailty. We want to look at them in the way that Jesus taught us to hope that such a vision will offer us a safe way to travel on earth." If, as Henri says, the Beatitudes are a self-portrait of Jesus, they fail to describe most of us!

Nouwen's theology of downward mobility is certainly not a popular one in our society, where our value is usually determined by success, popularity, and influence. Try telling an Olympic athlete that those who fail to win any medals are just as good as those who win the gold! In *Finding My Way Home* we find, "When you win and receive a prize, you know there is somebody who lost. But this is not so in the heart of God. If you are chosen in the heart of God, you have eyes to see the chosenness of others."

Nouwen reminds us that our time on earth is very brief, but that we were loved by God before we were born and will continue to be loved by God after we die. He writes, "This brief lifetime is my opportunity to receive love, deepen love, grow in love, and give love." In *Finding My Way Home* we discover that God's "power" is not about worldly success, but about the fruitfulness and the "transforming power of love." As we deepen our understanding of the power of love, we grow in freedom from fear. Our final journey home becomes an "exodus" in which "we leave this world for full communion with God."

Henri Nouwen made his final journey home four years ago, leaving a rich legacy behind. He lived his life with his eyes and heart on Jesus, and like Jesus he lived his life faithfully, passionately, and authentically and made his life abundantly fruitful through his death. This remarkable book inspires us to walk the same path in confidence as we, too, seek to find our way home.

WENDY WILSON GREER
President, Henri Nouwen Society

New York City
September 2000

Preface

As I hurried past, Henri invariably stopped when a homeless person accosted us on the street asking for money. Not only did he find some money to share from his pocket, but also he generally took time to speak to the person, ask some questions, and listen to the story. The sight of a brother's plight didn't repulse him nor did he seem to be the least bit afraid of some quite wild-looking people who inhabited the streets. But he was touched by the story of each person and in the days following, Henri often remembered the person by name during his celebration of the Eucharist. In looking beyond I had adapted to our society's reaction and I no longer "saw" the homeless person. Henri stopped. He felt akin to the homeless because Henri was deeply conscious of his longing for "home."

Finding My Way Home: Pathways to Life and the Spirit is a book that allows Henri to speak about our collective sense of homelessness today and the universal thirst for the experience of truly being at home. Three essays, "The Path of Power," "The Path of Peace," and "The Path of Waiting," first published in 1995 by the Crossroad Publishing Company, are combined in this volume along with a new article, "The Path of Living and Dying" from unpublished sources.

I remember how touched I was when I first read "The Path of Power." In his unique way Henri uses his three-point approach, but this time he chooses the same point twice for two very different descriptions of the same word! Under the heading of "Power," he outlines the destructive nature of economic and political power and, worse still, the misuse of religious power. It stings. For the second heading, "Powerlessness," he goes to the opposite extreme and describes how our God, in the form of Jesus, chose downward mobility to invite us to a life of intimacy with God. Then Henri chooses "Power" again for the heading of the third section, where he brilliantly reveals God's power as the power of love that engenders in us creativity, leadership, and new initiatives for the kingdom. This "second" power, connected with the portrait of Jesus painted in the Beatitudes, is ours to claim and wield. On the spiritual journey home, our very weakness is power.

In "The Path of Peace" Henri shares the lessons in wisdom he learned from Adam, his friend and mentor in the L'Arche Daybreak community. Henri experienced something with Adam that had never happened to him before, and this experience sent Henri searching for the sources of Adam's peace. Himself touched by Adam's peace, Henri also saw peace flowing from Adam's heart into the hearts of those around him. Adam was an unusual teacher who impressed Henri with the startling beauty of just being, of being present to another without the necessity of words, of being rooted in relationships more than in the mind, and of not fearing to be interdependent. Adam, Henri's quiet guide, leads us to deep wells of peace.

"The Path of Waiting" exposes in our culture a deep fear of the unknown and our need to control it as much as possible. This is in contrast to Zechariah and Elizabeth in the early nativity narratives, who hoped and waited for a child who was given to them only in their old age. Mary, the Mother of Jesus, and Simeon, living many years in the Temple, chose to wait for the full revelation of the Promise of God. Henri sees all our waiting as our waiting for God. But he also enlightens us with the waiting of God for us. Waiting for Henri is not a painful or passive experience but a chance to feel fully alive and active. By being present to the moment, by waiting together and not alone, and by transforming our wishes into hopes, we learn to "wait patiently in expectation."

"The Path of Living and Dying" is taken from the talk Henri gave to the National Catholic HIV/AIDS Conference in Chicago and an interview that Henri gave to *Crosspoint* magazine. As I was putting the material together I was surprised by the urgency of Henri's call to us to believe and accept our true identity as beloved children of God. Over and over again he says that Jesus heard and believed the words spoken at his baptism, "You are my beloved son. My favor rests on you." Henri is urging us to listen in our hearts for the same words so that we know and accept the truth of our lives, because living in the world as beloved sons and daughters of God is not the same as just living in the world. Henri gently guides the reader to dream not so much for success as for fruitfulness because fruitfulness extends beyond success, beyond weakness or diminishment, and even beyond death itself.

Because the material for *The Path of Living and Dying* was not Henri's written word, I confess, as editor, to taking some liberties with it in an effort to make it more coherent. As I did so, I read other texts of Henri's written word and I drew on them as well. I believe that the text is true to Henri's thought.

Finding My Way Home is an inspiration for the spiritual journey. It names the powers that seduce us to a life of unfulfilled self-seeking, as well as describing some practical choices to keep us on the path of meaning and faithfulness. To read it is to experience what Henri would call, "finding home on the way home."

SUE MOSTELLER,
Literary Executrix

Henri Nouwen Literary Centre
L'Arche Daybreak
August 2000

Acknowledgments

This book is the brainchild of Gwendolin Herder at the Crossroad Publishing Company. She thought that instead of just having the individual booklets entitled *Path of Power*, *Path of Peace*, and *Path of Waiting*, we should revise the texts and put them into one volume about pathways to life and the Spirit. Together the essays enhance each other and make a coherent spiritual book. I'm thankful for Gwendolin's creative initiative.

Tim Jones came to the Literary Centre to do research for his personal project, but when I told him that I needed new and unpublished material for one more Path in the Spirit, he went to work for me! He not only found some good material, but he also gave me some ideas about how it would complement the other Path. I am deeply grateful to him for his work and enthusiasm.

Kathy Christie was Henri's administrative assistant for

the last four years before his death. With remarkable love and skill she managed the many facets of Henri's life and publishing, and she was deeply shocked by Henri's sudden death. However, she didn't skip a beat when he died but continued at her desk, calling people and comforting them and listening to their stories. After Henri's death she welcomed me to the office and together we launched the Henri Nouwen Literary Centre. As this book goes to press we are concluding four wonderful and fruitful years of working there together. Kathy helped in the preparation of this book, not only by typing and retyping the material, but also by reading my revisions and giving me wise and helpful feedback. Kathy is a living example of someone who walks life's pathways with intention and compassion. Her love, support, work, and care have been invaluable.

Maureen Wright, who now manages the Henri Nouwen Literary Centre, also typed and retyped material for the book. She gave critical feedback as well about the way I put the material together for "The Path of Living and Dying." I have deep gratitude for her work and for her support.

Paul McMahon at the Crossroad Publishing Company worked with me on the publication of this work. Our mutual consultations were a support to me. He was also very kind to extend the deadline when I was having trouble meeting it.

I'm deeply grateful to each one and especially to Henri, who wrote the texts that have inspired me.

S. M.

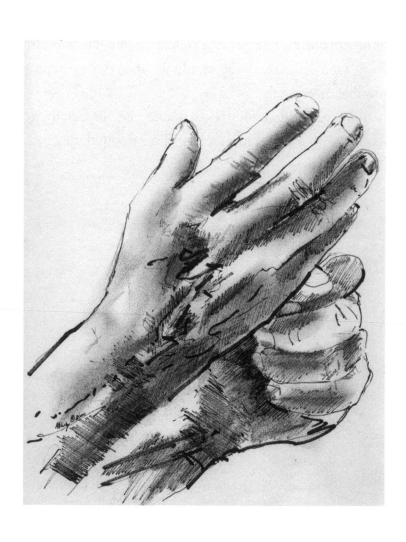

The Path of
Power

Sitting in a plane and looking down on the broad landscapes—the rivers, lakes, and mountains—and seeing the winding roads and little villages spread out over the earth, I wonder why it is so hard for people to live peacefully together. The astronauts seeing our blue planet from their space shuttle were so overwhelmed by its beauty that it seemed impossible for them to believe that its inhabitants were busy destroying their own home and killing each other through war and exploitation.

Distance sometimes helps us to get a sharper vision of our human condition and to raise some very good critical questions!

Let us take a look at our world from a distance, not from the physical distance of a plane or a space vehicle, but from the spiritual distance of our faith. Let us look at ourselves, at our humanity, from above and with the eyes of God. Jesus always looked at the human condition from above and tried to teach us to look as he did. "I come from above," he said, "and I want you to be reborn from above so that you will be able to see with new eyes."

This is what theology is about. It is looking at reality with the eyes of God. And there is so much to look at: land and sky; sun, stars, and moon; women, men, and children; continents, countries, cities and towns, and countless very specific issues in the past, present, and future. That's why there are so many "theologies." The sacred Scriptures help us to look at the rich variety of all creation with the eyes of God and so to discern the ways to live.

The path of power is really about a theology of weakness. We want to look with God's eyes at our experience of brokenness, limitedness, woundedness, and frailty. We want to look at them in the way that Jesus taught us to hope that such a vision will offer us a safe way to travel on earth. I will focus on three words: "power," "powerlessness," and "power." I first want to explore the power that oppresses and destroys. Then I want to show how power is disarmed through powerlessness, and finally I want to proclaim the true power that liberates, reconciles, and heals.

Power

I. When God looks at our world, God must weep. God must weep because the lust for power has entrapped and corrupted the human spirit. In the news and even in our families and ourselves we see that instead of gratitude there is resentment, instead of forgiveness there is revenge, instead of healing there is wounding, instead of compassion there is competition, instead of cooperation there is violence, and instead of love there is immense fear.

God must weep when God looks at our beautiful planet and sees thousands of maimed bodies lying on the battlefields, lonely children roaming the streets of big cities, prisoners locked behind bars and thick walls, mentally ill men and women wasting their time in the wards of large institutions, and millions of people dying from starvation and neglect. God must weep because God knows the agony and anguish we have brought upon ourselves by wanting to take our destiny in our own hands and lord it over others.

When we look around and within us with the eyes

of God, it is not hard to see the all-pervading lust for power. Why are Serbs and Moslems killing each other? Why are Protestants and Catholics throwing bombs at each other? Why is the president murdered, the prime minister kidnapped, and why do political leaders commit suicide?

Let's look into our own hearts! Aren't we constantly concerned with whether we are noticed or not, appreciated or not, rewarded or not? Aren't we always asking ourselves whether we are better or worse, stronger or weaker, faster or slower than the one who stands beside us? Haven't we, from elementary school on, experienced most of our fellow human beings as rivals in the race for success, influence, and popularity? And ... aren't we so insecure about who we are that we will grab any, yes any, form of power that gives us a little bit of control over who we are, what we do, and where we go?

When we are willing to look at things through God's eyes, we soon see that what is happening in Bosnia, South Africa, Ireland, or Los Angeles is not so far away from what is happening in our own hearts. As soon as our own safety is threatened we grab for the first stick or gun available and we say that *our* survival is what really counts, even when thousands of others are not going to make it.

I know my sticks and my guns! Sometimes it is a friend with more influence than I, sometimes it is money or a degree, sometimes it is a little talent that others don't have, and sometimes it is a special knowledge, or a hidden memory, or even a cold stare...and I will grab it quickly and without much hesitation when I need it to stay in control. Before I fully realize it I have pushed my friends away, perhaps wounding them in the process.

God looks at us and weeps because wherever we use power to give us a sense of ourselves, we separate ourselves from God and each other, and our lives become *diabolic,* in the literal meaning of that word: *divisive.*

II. But there is something worse than our exercise of economic and political power. It is religious power. When God looks at our world, God not only must weep but must also be angry—angry because many of us who pray, offer praise, and call out to God, "Lord,

Lord!" arc also corrupted by power. In anger God says: "These people honor me only with lip service, while their hearts are far from me. Their reverence of me is worthless; the lessons they teach are nothing but human commandments" (Isa. 29:13).

The most insidious, divisive, and wounding power is the power used in the service of God. The number of people who "have been wounded by religion" overwhelms me. An unfriendly or judgmental word by a minister or priest, a critical remark in church about a certain lifestyle, a refusal to welcome people at the table, an absence during an illness or death, and countless other hurts often remain longer in people's memories than other more world-like rejections. Thousands of separated and divorced men and women, numerous gay and lesbian people, and all of the homeless people who felt unwelcome in the houses of worship of their brothers and sisters in the human family have turned away from God because they experienced the use of power when they expected an expression of love.

The devastating influence of power in the hands of God's people becomes very clear when we think of the

The most insidious, divisive,
and wounding power
is the power used
in the service of God.

crusades, the pogroms, the policies of apartheid, and the long history of religious wars up to these very days. It might be harder though to realize that many contemporary religious movements create the fertile soil for these immense human tragedies to happen again.

In these days of great economic and political uncertainty, one of the greatest temptations is to use our faith as a way to exercise power over others and thereby supplant God's commandments with human commandments.

It is easy to understand why so many people have turned away in disgust from anything vaguely connected with religion. When power is used to proclaim good news, good news very soon becomes bad, very bad news. And that's what I believe causes God's anger.

But God looks at our world not only with sad or angry eyes; God's mercy is far greater than God's sadness and anger. As the Psalmist says: "God's anger lasts but a moment" (Ps. 30:5). In an all-embracing mercy God chooses to disarm the power of evil through powerlessness—God's own powerlessness.

Powerlessness

I. What was and is God's response to the diabolic power that rules the world and destroys people and their lands? The answer is a deep and complete mystery because God chose powerlessness. God chose to enter into human history in complete weakness. That divine choice forms the center of the Christian faith. In Jesus of Nazareth, the powerless God appeared among us to unmask the illusion of power, to disarm the prince of darkness who rules the world, and to bring the divided human race to a new unity. It is through total and unmitigated powerlessness that God shows us divine mercy. The radical, divine choice is the choice to reveal glory, beauty, truth, peace, joy, and, most of all, love in and through the complete divestment of power. It is very hard—if not impossible—for us to grasp this divine mystery. We keep praying to the "almighty and powerful God." But all might and power is absent from the one who reveals God to us saying: "When you see me you see the Father." If we truly want to love God, we have to look at the man of Nazareth, whose life was wrapped in weakness. And his weakness opens for us the way to the heart of God.

People with power do not invite intimacy. We fear people with power. They can control us and force us to do what we don't want to do. We look up to people with power. They have what we do not have and can give or refuse to give, according to their will. We envy people with power. They can afford to go where we cannot go and do what we cannot do. But God's power is something entirely opposite. God does not want us to be afraid, distant, or envious. God wants to come close, very close, so close that we can rest in the intimacy of God as children in their mother's arms.

Therefore God became a little baby. Who can be afraid of a little baby? A tiny little baby is completely dependent on its parents, nurses, and caregivers. Yes, God wanted to become so powerless as to be unable to eat or drink, walk or talk, play or work without many people's help. Yes, God became dependent on human beings to grow up and live among us and proclaim the good news. Yes, indeed, God chose to become so powerless that the realization of God's own mission among us became completely dependent on us. How can we fear a baby we rock in our arms, how can we look up to a baby that is so little and fragile, how can we be envious of a baby who only smiles at us in response to our tenderness? That's the mystery of the incarnation. God became human, in no way different from other human beings, to break through the walls of power in total weakness. That's the story of Jesus.

And how did that story end? It ended on a cross, where the same human person hangs naked with nails through his hands and feet. The powerlessness of the manger has become the powerlessness of the cross. People jeer at him, laugh at him, spit in his face, and shout: "He saved others; he cannot save himself! He is the King of Israel; let him come down from the cross now, and we will believe in him" (Matt. 27:42). He hangs there, his flesh torn apart by lead-filled whips, his heart broken by the rejection of his friends and abuse from his enemies, his mind tortured by anguish, his spirit shrouded in the darkness of abandonment—total weakness, total powerlessness. That's how God chose to reveal to us the divine love, bring us back into an embrace of

God became human,
in no way different
from other human beings,
to break through the walls of power
in total weakness.

compassion, and convince us that anger has been melted away in endless mercy.

II. But there is more to be said about God's powerlessness as it is revealed in Jesus of Nazareth. There is not only a powerless birth and a powerless death, but—strange as it may seem—a powerless life.

Jesus, the powerless child of God, is blessed in powerlessness. When, after a long hidden life in Nazareth, Jesus begins his ministry, he first offers us a self-portrait. "Blessed are the poor," he said. Jesus is poor, not in control, but marginal in his society. What good can come from Nazareth?

"Blessed are the gentle," he said. Jesus does not break the bruised reed. He always cares for the little ones.

"Blessed are those who mourn," he said. Jesus does not hide his grief, but lets his tears flow when his friend dies and when he foresees the destruction of his beloved Jerusalem.

"Blessed are those who hunger and thirst for justice," he said. Jesus doesn't hesitate to criticize injustice and to defend the hungry, the dying, and the lepers.

"Blessed are the merciful," he said. Jesus doesn't always call for revenge but heals always and everywhere.

"Blessed are the pure in heart," he said. Jesus remains focused only on what is necessary and does not allow his attention to be divided by many distractions.

"Blessed are the peacemakers," he said. Jesus does not stress differences, but reconciles people as brothers and sisters in one family.

"Blessed are those who are persecuted," he said. Jesus does not expect success and popularity, but knows that rejections and abandonment will make him suffer.

The Beatitudes give us Jesus' self-portrait. It is the portrait of the powerless God. It is also the portrait we glimpse wherever we see the sick, the prisoners, the refugees, the lonely, the victims of sexual abuse, the people with AIDS, and the dying. It is through their powerlessness that we are called to become brothers and sisters. It is through their powerlessness that we are called to deepen our bonds of friendship and love. It is through their powerlessness that we are challenged to lay down our weapons, offer each other forgiveness, and make peace. And it is through their powerlessness that we are constantly reminded of Jesus' words: "You foolish people, is it not necessary to suffer and so enter into glory?" Indeed, God's powerlessness and the powerlessness of the human race of which God became part has become the door to the house of love.

Power

I. Our world is ruled by diabolic powers that divide and destroy. In and through the powerless Jesus, God disarmed these powers. However, this mystery confronts us with a new and very hard question: how do we live in this world as witnesses to a powerless God and build the kingdom of love and peace?

Does powerlessness mean that we are doomed to be doormats for our power-hungry society? Does it mean that it is good to be soft, passive, subservient—always allowing the powers of darkness to dominate our lives? Does it mean that economic weakness, organizational weakness, physical and emotional weaknesses have now, suddenly, become virtues? Does it mean that people who are poorly prepared for their tasks can now brag about their poverty as a blessing that calls for gratitude? When we read Paul's words, "My strength is made perfect in weakness" (2 Cor. 12:9), do we imagine that we are dealing with a weakling who uses his low self-esteem as an argument to proclaim the gospel?

We touch here on one of the most dangerous traps of a theology of weakness. When we can become free from the enslaving powers of the world only by being enslaved by weakness, it seems a lot better to stay on the side of Satan than on the side of God. If a theology of weakness becomes a theology for weaklings, then such a theology is a comfortable excuse for incompetence, submissiveness, self-denigration, and defeat in all fields!

This is far from a theoretical possibility. Not seldom is financial, intellectual, and spiritual weakness interpreted as a divine privilege; not seldom is competent medical or psychological help delayed or avoided in the conviction that it is better to suffer for God than not to suffer; not seldom is careful planning, aggressive fundraising, and intelligent strategizing for the future frowned on as a lack of faithfulness to the ideal of powerlessness. Not seldom have the sick, the poor, the handicapped, and

"My strength is made perfect in weakness." (2 COR. 12:9)

all those who suffer been romanticized as God's privileged children, without much support to free them from their fate.

Nietzsche rightly criticized a theology of weakness. For him it was a theology that kept the poor in their poverty and gave the rulers of the religious establishment a chance to keep their "faithful" in a state of subservient obedience. Indeed, there is a spirituality of powerlessness, of weakness, of littleness that can be extremely dangerous, especially in the hands of those who feel they are called to speak and to act in God's name. Of them, Jesus says: "They tie up heavy burdens and lay them on people's shoulders, but they will not lift a finger to move them" (Matt. 23:4).

A theology of weakness challenges us to look at weakness not as a worldly weakness that allows us to be manipulated by the powerful in society and church, but as a total and unconditional dependence on God that opens us to be true channels of the divine power that heals the wounds of humanity and renews the face of the earth. The theology of weakness claims power, God's power, the all-transforming power of love.

Indeed, a theology of weakness is a theology that shows a God weeping for the human race entangled in its power games and angry that these same power games are so greedily used by so-called religious people. Indeed, a theology of weakness is a theology that shows how God unmasks the power games of the world and the church by entering into history in complete powerlessness. But a theology of weakness wants, ultimately, to show that God offers us, human beings, the divine power to walk on the earth confidently with heads erect.

II. God is powerful. Jesus doesn't hesitate to speak about God's power. He says: "In truth I tell you, there are some standing here who will not taste death before they see the kingdom of God come with power" (Matt. 9:2). Wherever Jesus went there was the experience of divine power. Luke writes: "Everyone in the crowd was trying to touch him because power came out of him that cured them all" (Luke 6:19). When a woman who had suffered from a hemorrhage for twelve years touched the fringe of Jesus' cloak, trusting that Jesus would cure her, Jesus said, "Someone touched me, I felt that power has gone out from me" (Luke 8:46). Jesus was filled with God's power. Jesus claims for himself the power to forgive sins, the power to heal, the power to call to life, yes, all power. The final words he directs to his friends are full of this conviction. He says: "All power in heaven and on earth has been given to me. Go, therefore, make disciples of all nations" (Matt. 28:12–19).

Power is claimed, and power is given. In and through the powerless Jesus, God wants to empower us, give us the power that Jesus had, and send us out—to cast out demons, to heal the sick, to call the dead to life, to reconcile the estranged, to create community, and to build the kingdom of God.

A theology of weakness is a theology of divine em-powering. It is not a theology for weaklings but a theology for men and women who claim for themselves the power of love that frees them from fear and enables them to put their light on the lampstands and do the work of the kingdom.

Yes, we are poor, gentle, mourning, hungry and thirsty for justice, merciful, pure of heart, peacemakers, and always persecuted by a hostile world. But we are no weaklings, no doormats! The kingdom of heaven is ours, the earth our inheritance. We are comforted, have our fill, experience mercy, are recognized as God's children and ... see God. That's power, real power, power that comes from above.

The movement from power through strength to power through powerlessness is our call. As fearful, anxious, insecure, and wounded people we are tempted constantly to grab the little bit of power that the world around us offers, left and right, here and there, now and then. These bits of power make us little puppets jerked up and down on strings until we are dead. But insofar as we dare to be baptized in powerlessness, always moving toward the poor who do not have such power, we are plunged right into the heart of God's endless mercy. We are free to reenter our world with the same divine power with which Jesus came, and we are able to walk in the valley of darkness and tears, unceasingly in communion with God, with our heads erect, confidently standing under the cross of our life.

It is this power that engenders leaders for our communities, women and men who dare to take risks and take

*The movement
from power through strength
to power through powerlessness
is our call.*

new initiatives. It is this power that enables us to be not only gentle as doves, but also as clever as serpents in our dealings with governments and church agencies. It is this power that enables us to talk straight and without hesitation about sharing money with those who have financial resources, to call men and woman to radical service, to challenge people to make long-term commitments in the world of human services, and to keep announcing the good news everywhere at all times. It is this divine power that makes us saints—fearless—who can make all things new.

Conclusion

How do we keep moving from dividing power to uniting power, from destructive power to healing power, from paralyzing power to enabling power?

Let me suggest three choices, all of them disciplines supporting us to look at our humanity and our personal lives from above and with the eyes of God.

The first discipline is to focus always on the poor who are close to us and in our world. We ask ourselves:

"Where are the men, women, and children who are waiting for us to reach out to them?" Poverty in all its forms, physical, intellectual, and emotional, is not decreasing. To the contrary, the poor are everywhere around us and beyond—more than ever. As the powers of darkness show their hideous intentions with increasing crudeness, the weeping of the poor becomes louder and louder and their misery more and more visible. We who yearn for peace must strive to keep listening and to keep looking. We must not run away from this painful sight.

The second discipline is to trust that God gives us what we need to truly care for the poor that are given to us. We choose to trust that we will have the financial, emotional, and physical support we need, when we need it, and to the degree that we need it. I am convinced that we are people who are ready to help with money, time, and talent. But we are often afraid to enter into the chaos surrounding situations of poverty, and we will remain paralyzed unless we dare to take new risks. If we need to have all our bases covered before we move into action, then nothing exciting ever happens, but if we dare to take a few crazy risks because God asks us to do so, many doors that we didn't even know existed open before us.

The third discipline is the hardest one. It is the discipline to be surprised not by suffering but by joy. As we grow old, we will have to stretch out our arms, be guided and led to places we would rather not go. What was true for Peter will be true for us. There is suffering ahead of us, immense suffering, a suffering that will continue to tempt us to think that we have chosen the wrong road and that others were more shrewd than we were. But don't be surprised by pain. Be surprised by joy, be surprised by the little flower that shows its beauty in the midst of a barren desert, and be surprised by the immense healing power that keeps bursting forth like springs of fresh water from the depth of our pain.

And so, with an eye focused on the poor, a heart trusting that we will get what we need, and a spirit always surprised by joy, we will exercise true power and walk through this valley of darkness performing and witnessing miracles. God's power becomes ours and goes out from us wherever we go and to whomever we meet.

Let me conclude with a little story about John and

Be surprised by joy,
be surprised by the little flower
that shows its beauty
in the midst of a barren desert.

Sandy. John and Sandy are two very simple people. We all have Johns and Sandys among us. One day John said to Sandy: "We have never had an argument. Let us have an argument like other people have." Sandy asked: "But how can we start an argument?" John answered: "It is very simple. I take a brick and say: 'It is mine,' and then you say: 'No it is mine,' and then we have an argument." So they sat down and John took a brick and said: "This brick is mine." Sandy looked gently at him and said: "Well, if it is yours take it." And so they could not have an argument.*

As long as we keep bricks in our hands and speak about mine and thine, our little power games gradually will escalate into big power games, and our big power games will lead to hatred, violence, and war. Looking at our lives from below, our fears and insecurities lead us to grab bricks wherever we can. But when we dare to let go of our bricks, empty our hands, and raise them up to the One who is our true refuge and our true stronghold, our poverty opens us to receive power from above, power that heals, power that will be a true blessing for ourselves and our world.

---

*This story is an adaptation of a story from the desert fathers.

The Path of
Peace

H ow to write about peace? During the past years my own life has gone through so many changes that I have lost much of my self-confidence. A few years ago it seemed rather easy to get up in front of many people and give them some suggestions about how to be people of peace. I was able to do that with a certain ease and with the conviction that I had something important to say.

As I prepare this essay, however, I experience a deep inner emptiness, a sense of futility in regard to words, even despair about saying something meaningful about peace, peacemaking, or a spirituality of peace. I feel tempted to call the whole thing off because my poverty seems too paralyzing.

I resist these feelings and decide to share my inadequacy, trusting that God does not want me to hide from it or to hide it from you. In the past I have often said that prayer, resistance, and community are the three core aspects of peace work. I still believe that this is true, but today I question the value of saying or writing it because I wonder if these concepts generate what they express. I am no longer as sure as I was before. I am no longer sure of the use of any words in helping us to become the people God calls us to be.

How then do I proceed? After agonizing over this question, I will begin with a little story about my present life and try to highlight my insights into those aspects of the peace of Jesus that we search to discover.

Some years ago I moved from Harvard to Daybreak, that is, from an institution for the best and the brightest to a community where people with an intellectual disability live. Daybreak, close to Toronto, is part of an international federation of communities called L'Arche—the Ark—where people with a mental handicap and their assistants try to live together in the spirit of the Beatitudes. I live in a house with six people with disabilities and three other assistants. None of the assistants is specially trained to work with people with a mental handicap, but we receive enormous support from doctors, psychiatrists, behavioral management people, social workers, and physiotherapists in our town.

When there are not special crises, we live together as a family, gradually forgetting who is handicapped and who is not. We are simply John, Bill, Trevor, Raymond,

Adam, Rose, Steve, Jan, Naomi, and Henri. We all have our gifts, our struggles, our strengths and weaknesses. We eat together, play together, pray together, and go out together. We all have our own preferences with regard to work, food, and movies, and we all have our problems in getting along with someone in the house, whether handicapped or not. We laugh a lot. We cry a lot too. Sometimes we do both at the same time.

Every morning when I say, "Good morning, Raymond," he growls back at me, "I am not awake yet. Saying good morning to everyone each day is unreal!" Last Christmas Eve Trevor wrapped marshmallows in silver paper as peace gifts for everyone, and during the Christmas dinner he climbed on a chair, lifted his glass, and said, "Ladies and gentlemen, this is not a celebration, this is Christmas."

When one of the men, speaking on the phone with someone, was bothered by the cigarette smoke of an assistant, he looked up and pleaded, "Stop smoking! I can't hear." Every dinner guest, upon arrival, is asked by Bill, "Hey, tell me, what is a turkey in suspense?" When the newcomer confesses ignorance, Bill, with a big grin on his face, says, "I'll tell you tomorrow." Then he laughs so loudly that the visitor has to laugh with him whether he or she finds the joke funny or not so funny.

This is L'Arche; this is Daybreak; this is the family of ten I am living with day in and day out. What can life in this family of a few poor people reveal about the peace of Christ for which we are searching? Let me tell you the story of Adam, one of the ten people in our home, and let him become the silent spokesperson of the peace that is not of this world.

Never having worked with disabled people before coming into this community, I was not only apprehensive but also even afraid to enter this unfamiliar world. This fear did not lessen when I was invited to work directly with Adam. When I first met Adam I was not aware of his amazing beauty and depth. I recognized at once that he was the weakest member of our small family. He is twenty-five years old, and he cannot speak, cannot dress or undress himself, cannot walk alone or eat without much help. He does not cry or laugh and only occasionally makes eye contact. His back isn't very straight and sometimes his movements seem distorted.

He suffers from severe epilepsy and, notwithstanding heavy medication, there are few days without "grand mal" seizures. Sometimes, as he grows suddenly rigid, he utters a painful groan, and on a few occasions I have seen a big tear coming down his cheek. It takes me about an hour and a half to waken Adam, give him his medication, walk him into his bath, undress him, wash him, shave him, brush his teeth, dress him, walk him to the kitchen, give him his breakfast, put him in his wheelchair, and bring him to his Day Program, where he spends most of the day doing therapeutic exercises, resting, or going for a coffee.

When a grand mal seizure occurs during this sequence of activities, much more time is needed, and he often has to return to sleep to regain some of the energy lost during a seizure.

I tell you all of this not to give you a nursing report but to share with you something quite intimate. After a month of working this way with Adam, something started to happen to me that never happened before. This amazing and special young man, who at first glance by many outsiders is considered deeply handicapped, an embarrassment, or a burden for caregivers, started to become my dearest companion.

As my fears of making a mistake or of hurting Adam gradually decreased and as I became more relaxed with his routine, a love started to grow within me. It was so full of tenderness and affection that most of my other daily tasks seemed boring and superficial compared with the hours spent with Adam. Out of what I initially saw as his broken body and broken mind a most beautiful human being emerged, offering me a much greater gift than I would ever be able to offer him. It is hard for me to find adequate words for this experience of coming to know him, but somehow Adam very slowly revealed to me who he was and who I was and how we could love each other.

As I lifted his naked body into the bathwater, made big waves to let the water run fast around his chest and neck, rubbed noses with him, and told him all sorts of stories about him and me, I knew that two friends were communicating far beyond the realm of thought or emotion. Deep speaks to deep, spirit speaks to spirit, and heart speaks to heart. I began to experience a mutuality of love not based so much on shared knowledge

Deep speaks to deep,
spirit speaks to spirit,
and heart speaks to heart.

or shared feelings, but on shared humanity. The longer I stayed with Adam the more clearly I recognized him as my gentle teacher, teaching me what no book, school, or professor could have ever taught me.

Am I romanticizing, making something beautiful out of something not beautiful at all, and projecting my hidden need to be a father on a deeply retarded person? Am I spiritualizing what in essence is an unnatural human condition? From my intellectual and psychological formation I am able to raise these questions. And I did raise them recently—during the writing of this story—when Adam's parents came for a visit. I asked them, "Tell me, during all the years you had Adam in your home, what did he give you?" His father smiled and said without a moment of hesitation: "He brought us peace . . . he is our peacemaker . . . our son of peace."

Let me, then, write about Adam's peace. It is indeed a peace that the world cannot give. I am moved by the simple privilege of giving words to the peace of one who has no words. The gift of peace hidden in Adam's utter weakness is a gift not of the world, but certainly for the world.

For Adam's gift to be recognized, someone has to lift it up, hand it on, and someone has to receive it. That, maybe, is the deepest vocation of the one who assists people with disabilities. It is helping them to share their gifts and helping others to recognize and receive their gifts.

Adam's particular gift of peace is rooted in his *being* and in his *heart* and it always calls forth *community*. Let us explore a little more deeply these three aspects of Adam's peace.

Rooted in His Being

Adam's peace is first of all a peace rooted in his *being*. Adam can do nothing. He is completely dependent on others every moment of his life. His gift is his pure *being with us*. Every evening when I run home to "do" Adam's routine, to help him with his supper and put him to bed, I realize that the best thing I can do for Adam is to simply "be" with him. I really believe that if Adam wants anything, it is that I "be" with him. Nothing more. And indeed I am surprised that this becomes my great joy: paying total attention to his breathing, his eating, his careful steps, looking at how he tries to lift a spoon to his mouth, or how he raises his left arm a little to make it easier for me to take off his shirt. I find myself always wondering about possible pains that he cannot express but that still ask for relief. I am simply here, present with my friend. How simple the truth that Adam teaches me, but how hard to live! Being is more important than doing.

Most of my past life has been built around the idea that my value depends on what I do. I made it through grade school, high school, and university. I earned my degrees and awards and I made my career. Yes, with many others I fought my way up to the lonely top of a little success, a little popularity, and a little power.

But as I sit beside the slow and heavily breathing Adam, I start seeing how violent my journey has been. This upward passage has been so filled with desires to be better than others, so marked by rivalry and competition, so pervaded with compulsions and obsessions, and so spotted with moments of suspicion, jealousy, resentment, and revenge. What I believed I was doing

Peace is not primarily about doing.
It is first of all the art of being.

was called "ministry." It was named "ministry of justice and peace," "ministry of forgiveness and reconciliation," "ministry of healing and wholeness," but there was disparity for me between the words and the experience. This experience causes me to ask myself, "When I work for peace and am as interested in success, popularity, and power as those who want war, what then is the real difference between us?" or "When the peace I work for is as much of this world as the war, and when as peacemakers we violate one another's deepest values, what other choices are there?"

In his silent way Adam keeps telling me, "Peace is not primarily about doing. It is first of all the art of being." I know he is right because after four months of being with Adam I am discovering in myself the beginning of an inner at-homeness that I didn't know before. I even feel the unusual desire to do a lot less and be a lot more, preferably with Adam.

As I cover him with his sheets and blankets and turn out the lights, I pray with Adam. He is always very quiet as if he knows that my praying voice sounds a little different from my speaking voice. I whisper in his ear: "May all the angels protect you," and he looks up at me from his pillow, seemingly aware of what I am saying to him. Since I began to pray with Adam I have also come to know better what prayer is about. Prayer is being with Jesus and simply spending time with him. Adam is teaching me that.

Rooted in His Heart

Somehow during the centuries we have come to believe that what makes us human is our mind. Even those unfamiliar with Latin know Seneca's definition of a human being as a reasoning animal: *rationale animal est homo.* To say, "True peace belongs to the heart," is such a radical statement in our culture and our society that only very vulnerable and gifted people, like Adam, seem to be able to communicate it! Adam's peace is not only a peace rooted in his being; it is a peace rooted in his heart.

Adam keeps revealing to me, over and over again and in his own clear way, that what makes us human is not primarily our minds but our hearts; it is not first of all our ability to think which gives us our particular identity in all of creation, but it is our ability to love. The one who sees Adam first as a disabled person misses the sacred mystery that Adam is fully capable of receiving and offering love. He is fully human, not a little bit human, not half human, not nearly human, but fully, completely human because Adam is all heart. And it is his heart that is made in the image and likeness of God. If this were not the case, how could I ever say to you that Adam and I love each other? How could I ever experience new life from simply being with him? How could I ever trust that moving away from my past, where I was teaching many men and women, to being with Adam as my teacher, is a real step forward? I am speaking here about something very, very real. It is about the hidden mystery of the primacy of the heart in our true identity as human beings.

Let me say here that by "heart" I do not mean the seat of human emotions in contrast to the mind as the seat of human thought. No, by heart I mean the center of our being where God comes to dwell with us and bring us the divine gifts of trust, hope, and love. The mind tries to understand, grasp problems, discern different aspects of reality, and probe the mysteries of life. The heart allows us to enter into relationships and experience that we are sons and daughters of God and of our parents, as well as brothers and sisters of one another. Long before our minds were able to exercise their potential, our hearts were developing trusting human relationships. And in fact I am convinced that these trusting human relationships even precede the moment of our birth.

Here we are touching the origin of the spiritual life. We sometimes think that the spiritual life is the last to come, following the development of the biological, emotional, and intellectual life. But living with Adam and reflecting on my experience with him makes me realize that God's loving spirit has touched us long before we can walk, feel, or talk. The spiritual life is given to us from the moment of our conception. It is the divine gift of love that constitutes the spiritual life and makes the human person able to reveal to others a presence much greater than oneself.

When I say that I believe deeply that Adam can give and receive love and that there is a true mutuality

Those with the deepest handicaps
are the true center of gravity
of our togetherness.

between us, I do not make a naïve psychological statement overlooking his severe handicaps. I am speaking
about a love between us that transcends thoughts and
feelings precisely because it is rooted in God's first love,
a love that precedes all human loves. The mystery of
Adam is that in his deep mental and physical brokenness
he has become so empty of all human pride that he has
become the preferable mediator of that first love poured
into his heart by God. Maybe this will help you see why
Adam is giving me a whole new understanding of God's
love for the poor and the oppressed. He is offering me a
new perspective on the well-known "preferential option"
for the poor.

The peace that flows from Adam's broken heart is
not of this world. It is not the result of political analy-
sis, roundtable debates, discernment of the signs of the
times, or well-thought-out strategies. All these activities of the mind have their role to play in the complex
process of peacemaking. But they all will become easily
perverted to a new way of war-making if they are not put
into the service of the divine peace that flows from the
hearts of those who are often called the poor in spirit.

Calling Forth Community

The third and most tangible quality of Adam's peace is that, while rooted more in being than in doing and more in the heart than in the mind, his is a peace that always calls forth community. One of the deepest insights gleaned from my life at L'Arche is that the people with a disability call us together as family, and that those with the deepest handicaps are the true center of gravity of our togetherness. Adam in his total vulnerability calls us together around him. And he turns my perspective of community formation upside down. The weakest members in our midst are, in fact, the assistants. We come from different countries—Brazil, the United States, Canada, and Holland—and our commitments are ambiguous at best. Some stay longer than others, but most move on after one or two years. Closer to the center of our community life are Raymond, Bill, John, and Trevor, who are relatively independent but cannot make it on their own and still need much help and attention. They are permanent members of the family. They are with us for life and they keep calling us to be present to them. They call us to be honest. Because of them and of their weakness we must find unity among us, so conflicts never last very long, tensions are talked out, and disagreements resolved. And right in the heart of our community are Rose and Adam, both deeply handicapped and needy, and the weaker of the two is Adam.

Adam is the weakest of us all, but without any doubt the strongest bond between us all. Because of Adam there is always someone home; because of Adam there is a quiet rhythm in the house; because of Adam there are moments of silence and quiet; because of Adam there are always words of affection, gentleness, and tenderness; because of Adam there is patience and endurance; because of Adam there are smiles and tears visible to all; because of Adam there is always space for mutual forgiveness and healing . . . yes, because of Adam there is peace among us. How otherwise could people from such different nationalities and cultures, people with such different characters and with such an odd variety of handicaps, whether mental or not, live together in peace?

Adam truly calls us together around him and molds this motley group of strangers into a family. Adam is our

"God chose those
who by human standards are fools
to shame the wise." (1 COR. 1:27–30)

true peacemaker. How mysterious are the ways of God: "God chose those who by human standards are fools to shame the wise; he chose those who by human standards are weak in order to shame the strong, those who by human standards are common and contemptible— indeed who count for nothing—to reduce to nothing all those who do count for something, so that no human being might feel boastful before God" (1 Cor. 1:27–30). Adam gives flesh to these words of Paul. He teaches me the true mystery of community.

Most of my adult life I have tried to show the world that I could do it on my own, that I needed others only to get me back on my lonely road. Those who have helped me helped me to become a strong, independent, self-motivated, creative man who would be able to survive in the long search for individual freedom. With many others, I wanted to become a self-sufficient star. And most of my fellow intellectuals joined me in that desire.

But all of us highly trained individuals are facing today a world on the brink of total destruction. And now we start to wonder how we might join forces to make peace! What kind of peace can this possibly be? How can we paint a portrait of people who all want to take the center seat? Who will build a beautiful church with people who are interested only in erecting the tower? Who can bake a birthday cake with people who want only to put the candles on? We all know the problem. When all want the honor of being the final peacemaker, there never will be peace.

Adam needs many people and nobody can boast of anything. Adam will never be "cured." His constant seizures even make it likely that medically things will only get worse. There are no successes to claim, and everyone who works with him does only a little bit. My part in his life is very, very small. Some cook for him, others do his laundry, some give him massages, others play music for him, take him for a walk, a swim, or a ride. Some look after his blood pressure and regulate his medicine; others look after his teeth.

Although with all this assistance Adam doesn't change and often seems to slip away in a state of total exhaustion, a community of peace has emerged around him. It is a community that certainly does not want to put its light under a basket, because the peace community that Adam has called forth is not there just for Adam, but for all who belong to Adam's race. It is a community that proclaims that God has chosen to descend among us as an infant in a stable, in complete weakness and vulnerability, and thus to reveal to us the glory of God.

Adam is gradually teaching me something about the peace that is not of this world. It is a peace not constructed by tough competition, hard thinking, and individual stardom, but rooted in simply being present to each other and working together in harmony, a peace that speaks about the first love of God by which we are all held safe, and a peace that keeps calling us to community in a fellowship of the weak. Adam has never said a word to me. He will never do so. But every night as I put him to bed I say "thank you" to him. How much closer can one come to the Word that became flesh and dwells among us?

I have told you about Adam and about Adam's peace. But you are not part of L'Arche, you do not live at Daybreak, you are not a member of Adam's family. Like me, however, you search for peace and want to find peace in your heart, your family, and your world. But looking around us in the world, we see concentration camps and refugee camps; we see overcrowded prisons; we see the burning of villages, genocidal actions, kidnappings, torture, and murder; we see starving children, neglected elderly, and countless men and women without food, shelter, or a job. We see people sleeping in the city streets, young girls and boys selling themselves for others' pleasure; we see violence and rape and the desperation of millions of fearful and lonely people.

Seeing all this, we realize that there is no peace in our world. And still . . . that is what our hearts desire most. You and I may have tried giving money, demonstrating, overseas projects, and many other things—but as we grow older we are faced with the fact that the peace we waited for still has not come. Something in us is in danger of growing cold, bitter, and resentful, and we are tempted to withdraw from it all and limit ourselves to the easier task of personal survival. But that is a demonic temptation.

I have told you about Adam and his peace to offer you a quiet guide with a gentle heart who gives you a

*Keep your eyes
on the prince of peace,
the one who doesn't cling
to his divine power.*

little light to guide you through this dark world. Adam does not solve anything. Even with all the support he receives, he cannot change his own utter poverty. As he grows older, he grows poorer and poorer and poorer. A little infection, an unhappy fall, an accidental swallowing of his own tongue during a seizure, and many other small incidents may take him suddenly away from us. When he dies, nobody will be able to boast about anything.

And still, what a light he brings! In Adam's name I therefore say to you: Do not give up working for peace. Always remember that the peace for which you work is not of this world. Do not let yourself be distracted by the great noises of war, the dramatic descriptions of misery, and the sensational expressions of human cruelty. The newspapers, movies, and war novels may make you numb, but they do not create in you a true desire for peace. They tend to create feelings of shame, guilt, and powerlessness, and these feelings are the worst motives for peace work.

Keep your eyes on the prince of peace, the one who doesn't cling to his divine power; the one who refuses to turn stones into bread, jump from great heights, and rule with great power; the one who says, "Blessed are the poor, the gentle, those who mourn, and those who hunger and thirst for righteousness; blessed are the merciful, the pure in heart, the peacemakers and those who are persecuted in the cause of uprightness" (see Matt. 5:3–11). See the one who touches the lame, the crippled, and the blind; the one who speaks words of forgiveness and encouragement; the one who dies alone, rejected, and despised. Keep your eyes on him who becomes poor with the poor, weak with the weak, and who is rejected with the rejected. That one, Jesus, is the source of all peace.

Where is his peace to be found? The answer is surprising but it is clear. In weakness. Few people are telling us this truth, but there is peace to be found in our own weakness, in those places of our hearts where we feel most broken, most insecure, most in agony, most afraid. Why there? Because in our weakness our familiar ways of controlling and manipulating our world are being stripped away and we are forced to let go from doing much, thinking much, and relying on our self-sufficiency.

Right there where we are most vulnerable, the peace that is not of this world is mysteriously hidden.

In Adam's name I say to you: Claim that peace that remains unknown to so many and make it your own. I say claim it because with that peace in your heart you will have new eyes to see and new ears to hear and gradually recognize that same peace in people and places where you would have least expected to find peace.

Not long ago I was in Honduras. It was my first time in Central America since I had come to Daybreak and become friends with Adam. I suddenly realized that I was a little less consumed by anger about the political manipulations, a little less distracted by the blatant injustices, and a little less paralyzed by the realization that the future of Honduras looks very dark. Visiting a severely handicapped man, Raphael, in the L'Arche community near Tegucigalpa, I saw the same peace I had seen in Adam. I also heard many stories about the gifts of joy offered by the poorest of the poor to the oh-so-serious assistants who came from France, Belgium, the United States, and Canada. From all this I know ever more clearly that peace is a gift of God, often hidden from

Peace is a gift of God,
often hidden from the wise
and the wealthy,
and revealed to those who feel
empty, inarticulate, and poor.

the wise and the wealthy and revealed to those who feel empty, inarticulate, and poor.

I am not saying that the questions about peace in Bosnia, Haiti, and Rwanda are no longer important. Far from it! I am only saying that the seeds of national and international peace are already mysteriously sown in the soil of our own pain and in the suffering of the poor. And I am convinced that we can truly trust these seeds, like the mustard seeds of the gospel that grow and produce large shrubs in which many birds of the air can find a place to rest.

As long as we imagine and live as if there is no peace in sight, and that it all depends on us to make it come about, we are on the road to self-destruction. But when we trust that the God of love has already given the peace we are searching for, we will see this peace breaking through the broken soil of our human condition and we will be able to let it grow fast and even heal the economic and political maladies of our time. With this trust in our hearts, we will be able to hear the words: "Blessed are the peacemakers, for they shall inherit the earth" (Matt. 5:9). It fills me with a special joy that all the Adams of this world are the first to receive this inheritance.

Conclusion

It is time to end, and somehow it feels hard to end because there are so many unspoken words, unexpressed feelings, and unrevealed mysteries. But I have to trust that you will know about them even when they have remained hidden. . . .

So many people today live in the night; a few live in the day. We all know about night and day, darkness and light. We know about it in our hearts; we know about it in our families and communities; we know about it in our world. The peace that the world does not give is the light that dispels some of this darkness. Every bit of that peace makes the day come!

Let me conclude with an old Hasidic tale that summarizes much of what I have tried to say.

The rabbi asked his students: "How can we determine the hour of dawn, when the night ends and the day begins?"

"Blessed are the peacemakers,
for they shall inherit the earth."

(MATT. 5:9)

One of the rabbi's students suggested: "When from a distance you can distinguish between a dog and a sheep?"

"No," was the answer of the rabbi.

"Is it when one can distinguish between a fig tree and a grapevine?" asked a second student.

"No," the rabbi said.

"Please tell us the answer, then," said the students.

"It is, then," said the wise teacher, "when you can look into the face of another human being and you have enough light in you to recognize your brother or your sister. Until then it is night, and darkness is still with us."

Let us pray for the light. It is the peace the world cannot give.

The Path of
Waiting

S OMETHING THAT HAS BEEN ON MY MIND for the past few years, which I sense is of importance to our lives, is the spirituality of waiting. I ponder it and I wonder what waiting means in the context of our spiritual lives.

I realize that a reflection on waiting from a spiritual perspective can be approached from two directions, namely, the waiting *for* God and the waiting *of* God. We are waiting. God is waiting. The beginning of Luke's Gospel sets the scene for my thoughts on the waiting for God, while the final chapters of the same Gospel provide the landscape for my reflections about the waiting of God. The story of Jesus' birth introduces us to five people who are waiting—Zechariah and Elizabeth, Mary, Simeon, and Anna. The story of Jesus' death and resurrection reveals to us a God who is waiting.

Our Waiting for God

In our personal lives, waiting is not a very popular pastime. Waiting is not something we anticipate or

---

Tapes of this material are available from Ave Maria Press (Notre Dame, IN 46556) or your local religious bookstore.

The story of Jesus'
death and resurrection
reveals to us a God who is waiting.

experience with great joy and gladness! In fact, most of us consider waiting a waste of time. Perhaps this is because the culture in which we live is basically saying, "Get going! Do something! Show you are able to make a difference! Don't just sit there and wait!" So, for us and for many people, waiting is a dry desert between where we are and where we want to be. We do not enjoy such a place. We want to move out of it and do something worthwhile.

In our particular historical situation, waiting is even more difficult because we are so fearful. One of the most pervasive emotions in the atmosphere around us is fear. We as a people are afraid—afraid of other people who may be different, afraid of inner or uncomfortable feelings, and also afraid of an unknown future. As fearful people we have a hard time waiting, because fear urges us to get away from where we are. If we find that we cannot flee, we may fight instead. We are aware of the many destructive acts that arise from our fear that something harmful will be done to us.

And if we take an even broader perspective—that not only ourselves as individuals or as a people, but also whole communities and nations fear being harmed—we can understand more clearly how hard it is to wait and how tempting it is to act. Right here are the roots of a "first strike" approach to others. Those who live in a world of fear are more likely to make aggressive, hostile, destructive responses than people who are not so frightened. The more afraid we are, the harder waiting becomes. That is why waiting is such an unpopular attitude for so many of us.

It impresses me to recognize that all the figures appearing on the first pages of Luke's Gospel are waiting. Zechariah and Elizabeth are waiting. Mary is waiting. Simeon and Anna, who were there at the Temple when Jesus was brought in, are waiting. The whole opening scene of the good news is filled with waiting people. And right from the beginning all these waiting people in some way or another hear the words, "Do not be afraid. I have something good to say to you." These words indicate that Zechariah, Elizabeth, Mary, Simeon, and Anna are waiting for something new and good to happen to them.

Let us look at these figures and see what they can teach us about the spirituality of waiting. Who are they and what do they have to fear? Besides being individuals loved by God, are they not also the representatives of waiting Israel? The Psalms are full of this kind of waiting. "My soul is waiting for the Lord. I count on God's word. My soul is longing for the Lord more than the guard for dawn. Let the guard count on the daybreak and Israel on the Lord. Because with the Lord there is mercy, and fullness of redemption" (Ps. 129:5–7, GRAIL). "My soul is waiting for the Lord"—that is the theme that reverberates all through the Hebrew Scriptures.

But not all who dwell in Israel are waiting. In fact we might say that the prophets criticized the people, at least in part, for giving all their attentiveness to what was coming. Waiting finally became the attitude of only the remnant of Israel, of that small group of Israelites that had remained faithful. The prophet Zephaniah says, "In your midst I will leave a humble and lowly people, and those who are left in Israel will seek refuge in the name of God. They will do no wrong, will tell no lies; and the perjured tongue will no longer be found in their mouths" (Zeph. 3:12–13, JB). It is the purified remnant of faithful people who are waiting. Elizabeth, Zechariah,

Mary, Simeon, and Anna are the representatives of that remnant. They have been able to wait, to be attentive, and to live in expectation.

Let us examine the lives of these men and women in order to see what the nature of their waiting is, and what the practice of their waiting is. Let us try to identify with them and discover how their waiting resembles ours and how we are called to wait with them.

The Nature of Waiting

Waiting, as we see it in the people on the first pages of the Gospel, is waiting with a sense of promise. "Zechariah, your wife Elizabeth is to bear you a son." "Mary, listen! You are to conceive and bear a son." "It had been revealed to him [Simeon] by the Holy Spirit that he would not see death until he had set eyes on the Christ of the Lord." (Luke 1:13, 31, and 2:26, JB). Those who were waiting had each received a promise that gave them courage and allowed them to wait. They received something that was at work in them, a seed that had started to grow.

*A waiting person is someone
who is present to the moment,
believing that this moment
is the moment.*

This is very important for us because we too can wait only if what we are waiting for has already begun for us. Waiting is never a movement from nothing to something. It is always a movement from something to something more. Zechariah, Elizabeth, Mary, Simeon, and Anna were living with a promise. It was a promise that nurtured them, fed them, and enabled them to stay where they were. By their waiting, the promise could gradually unfold and realize itself within them and through them.

Second, their waiting is active. Most of us consider waiting as something very passive, a hopeless state determined by events totally out of our hands. The bus is late? We cannot do anything about it, so we have to sit there and just wait. It is not difficult to understand the irritation people feel when somebody says, "Just wait." Words like that push us into passivity.

But there is none of this passivity in Scripture. Those who are waiting are waiting very actively. They know that what they are waiting for is growing from the ground on which they are standing. Right here is a secret for us about waiting. If we wait in the conviction that a seed has been planted and that something has already begun, it changes the way we wait. Active waiting implies being fully present to the moment with the conviction that something is happening where we are and that we want to be present to it. A waiting person is someone who is present to the moment, believing that this moment is *the* moment.

Zechariah, Elizabeth, Mary, Simeon, and Anna were present to the moment. That is why they could hear the angel. They were alert, attentive to the voice that spoke to them and said, "Don't be afraid. Something is happening to you. Pay attention."

A waiting person is a patient person. The word "patience" implies the willingness to stay where we are and live the situation out to the full in the belief that something hidden there will manifest itself to us. Patient living means to live actively in the present and wait there. Impatient people expect the real thing to happen somewhere else, and therefore they want to get away from the present situation and go elsewhere. For them the moment is empty. But patient people dare to stay where they are. Waiting, then, is not passive. It involves nurturing the growth of something growing within.

There is more. Waiting is also open-ended. Open-ended waiting is hard for us because we tend to wait for something that we wish to have, but we do not know if or when we will have it. It is not concrete. Much of our waiting is filled with wishes: "I wish that I had a job. I wish the weather were better. I wish the pain would go away." We are full of wishes, and our waiting easily gets entangled in those wishes. We want the future to go in a very specific direction, and if this does not happen we are disappointed and can even slip into despair. What will life be like if I do not get the things I wish for? One of the reasons we have such a hard time waiting is that we want to do the things that will make the desired events take place and thus satisfy our wishes. Here we realize how our wishes tend to be connected with our fears, and fear, of course, prevents us from allowing time in our lives for open-ended waiting. For this reason, a lot of our waiting is not open-ended. Instead, our waiting is a way of controlling the future.

But Zechariah, Elizabeth, Mary, Simeon, and Anna were not filled with wishes. They were filled with hope. Their hope was something very different. Their hope was trusting that fulfillment would come, but fulfillment according to the promises of God and not just according to their wishes. Hope is always open-ended.

Just imagine what Mary was actually saying in the words to the angel Gabriel, "I am the handmaid of the Lord. Let what you have said be done to me" (Luke 1:38, JB). She was saying, "I don't know what this all means, but I trust God and I trust you and I believe that good things will happen." She trusted so deeply that her waiting was open to all possibilities. She believed that when she listened carefully, she could trust what was going to happen.

I have found it very important in my own life to try to let go of my wishes and instead to live in hope. I am finding that when I choose to let go of my sometimes petty and superficial wishes and trust that my life is precious and meaningful in the eyes of God something really new, something beyond my own expectations begins to happen for me.

To wait with openness and trust is an enormously radical attitude toward life. It is choosing to hope that something is happening for us that is far beyond our own

*To wait with openness and trust
is an enormously radical attitude
toward life.*

imaginings. It is giving up control over our future and letting God define our life. It is living with the conviction that God molds us in love, holds us in tenderness, and moves us away from the sources of our fear.

Our spiritual life is a life in which we wait, actively present to the moment, expecting that new things will happen to us, new things that are far beyond our own imagination or prediction. This, indeed, is a very radical stance toward life in a world preoccupied with control.

The Practice of Waiting

How do we wait? Waiting together with family and friends is better than waiting alone. Waiting together is more human and more divine. One of the most beautiful passages of Scripture begins, "Mary set out at that time and went as quickly as she could to a town in the hill country of Judah. She went into Zechariah's house and greeted Elizabeth" (Luke 1:39–56, JB). It is the story of Mary's visit to Elizabeth just after she had received the promise of bearing a son. What happened when Mary received the words of promise? She went to Elizabeth. Something was happening to Elizabeth as well as to Mary. But how could they live that out?

I find the meeting of these two women very moving, because Elizabeth and Mary came together and enabled each other to wait. Mary's visit made Elizabeth aware of what she was waiting for. The child leapt for joy in her. Mary affirmed Elizabeth's waiting. And then Elizabeth said to Mary, "Blessed is she who believed that the promise made her by the Lord would be fulfilled" (Luke 1:45, JB). And Mary responded, "My soul proclaims the greatness of the Lord" (Luke 1:46, JB). She burst into joy herself. By being together these two women created space for each other to wait. They affirmed for each other that something was happening that was worth waiting for.

Here we see a model for the Christian family and the Christian community. Family and community are about support, celebration, and affirmation where we lift up what has already begun in us. The visit of Mary to Elizabeth is one of the Bible's most beautiful expressions of what it means to form community, to be together, gathered around a promise, affirming what is happening among us.

This is what prayer is all about too. Prayer is coming together around a promise. This is also what celebration is all about. It is lifting up and rejoicing with what is already there. This is what Eucharist is about. It is saying "Thanks" for the seed that has been planted. It is saying, "We are waiting for the Lord, who has already come."

The whole meaning of the family lies in offering each other a space and support to wait for what we have already seen. Christian community is the place where we keep the flame of hope alive among us and take it seriously so that it can grow and become stronger in us. In this way we can live with courage, trusting that there is a spiritual power in us when we are together that allows us to live in this world without surrendering to the powerful forces constantly seducing us toward despair. That is how we dare to say that God is a God of love even when we see hatred all around us. That is why we can claim that God is a God of life even when we see death and destruction and agony all around us. We say it together. We affirm it in each other. Waiting together, nurturing

Christian community
is the place where we keep
the flame of hope alive among us
and take it seriously
so that it can grow
and become stronger in us.

what has already begun, expecting its fulfillment—that is the meaning of marriage, friendship, community, and the Christian life.

Our waiting is always shaped by alertness to the Word of God that comes to us in such mysterious ways. It is waiting in the knowledge that Someone wants to address us. The question is, are we home? Are we at our address, ready to respond to the doorbell? We need to wait together to keep each other at home spiritually, so that when the Word comes it can become flesh in us. That is why the Book of God is always in the midst of those who gather. We read the Word so that the Word can become flesh and have a whole new life in us.

Simone Weil, a Jewish writer, said, "Waiting patiently in expectation is the foundation of the spiritual life." When Jesus speaks about the end of time, he speaks precisely about the importance of waiting. He says that nations will fight against nations and that there will be wars and earthquakes and misery. People will be in agony, and they will say, "The Christ is there! No, he is here!" Many will be confused, and many will be deceived. But Jesus says, you must stand ready, stay awake, stay tuned to the word of God, so that you will survive all that is going to happen and be able to stand confidently (*con-fide*, with trust) in the presence of God together in community (see Matt. 24). That is the attitude of waiting which allows us to be people who can live in a very chaotic world and survive spiritually.

God's Waiting for Us

But waiting is not always active like that of Zechariah and Elizabeth, Mary, and Simeon and Anna, who waited for God. In the passion and resurrection of Jesus we recognize the waiting of God. That is the second aspect of waiting that also deeply affects our spiritual lives. The end of Jesus' life reveals God as a waiting God, giving us an example of another kind of waiting. But let me start with a little story.

I was invited to visit a friend who was very sick. He was a man fifty-three years old who had lived a very active, useful, faithful, creative life. Actually, he was a social activist who had cared deeply for people, especially the poor. When he was fifty he discovered that he was suffering from cancer. During the three years that followed he became increasingly disabled.

When I came to him, he said to me, "Henri, here I am lying in this bed, and I don't even know how to think about being sick. My whole way of thinking about myself is in terms of action, in terms of doing things for people. My life is valuable because I've been able to do many things for many people. And suddenly, here I am, passive, and I can't do anything anymore.... Please help me to think about this situation in a new way. Please help me to think about my inability to do anything anymore in a way that won't drive me to despair. Help me to understand what it means that now all sorts of people are doing things to me over which I have no control."

As we talked I realized that he was constantly wondering, "How much can I still do?" Somehow my friend had learned to think about himself as a man who was worth only what he was doing. And so when he got sick, his hope seemed to rest on the idea that he might get better and return to what he had been doing. I realized, too, that this way of thinking was hopeless because he had cancer and was going to get worse and worse. He would die soon. If the spirit of my friend was dependent on how much he would still be able to do, what did I have to say to him?

In the context of these thoughts we read together a book called *The Stature of Waiting* by British author V. H. Vanstone.* Vanstone writes about Jesus' agony in the Garden of Gethsemane and his way to the cross. I want to draw on this powerful book in what follows. It helped my friend and me to understand better what it means to move from action to passion.

From Action to Passion

The central word in the story of Jesus' arrest is one I never thought much about. It is "to be handed over." That is what happened in Gethsemane. Jesus was handed over. Some translations say that Jesus was "betrayed," but the Greek says, "to be handed over." Judas handed Jesus over (see Mark 14:10). But the remarkable thing

---

*V. H. Vanstone, *The Stature of Waiting* (New York: Seabury Press, 1983).

is that the same word is used not only for Judas but also for God. God did not spare Jesus, but handed him over to benefit us all (see Rom. 8:32).

So this term "to be handed over" plays a central role in the life of Jesus. Indeed, this drama of being handed over divides the life of Jesus radically in two. The first part of Jesus' life is filled with activity. Jesus takes all sorts of initiatives. He speaks; he preaches; he heals; he travels. But immediately after Jesus is handed over, he becomes the one to whom things are being done. He's being arrested; he's being led to the high priest; he's being taken before Pilate; he's being crowned with thorns; he's being nailed on a cross. Things are being done to him over which he has no control. That is the meaning of passion—being the recipient of other people's actions.

It is important for us to realize that when Jesus says, "It is accomplished" (John 19:30), he does not simply mean, "I have done all the things I wanted to do." He also means, "I have allowed things to be done to me that needed to be done to me in order for me to fulfill my vocation." Jesus does not fulfill his vocation in action only, but also in passion. He doesn't fulfill his vocation

111

just by doing the things the Father sent him to do, but also by letting things be done to him.

Passion is a kind of waiting—waiting for what other people are going to do. Jesus went to Jerusalem to announce the good news to the people of that city. And Jesus knew that he was going to put a choice before them: Will you be my disciple, or will you be my executioner? There is no middle ground here. Jesus went to Jerusalem to put people in a situation where they had to say "Yes" or "No." That is the great drama of Jesus' passion: he had to wait for their response. What would they do? Betray him or follow him? In a way, his agony is not simply the agony of approaching death. It is also the agony of being out of control and of having to wait. It is the agony of a God who depends on us to decide how to live out the divine presence among us. It is the agony of the God who, in a very mysterious way, allows us to decide how God will be God. Here we glimpse the mystery of God's incarnation. God became human not only to act among us but also to be the recipient of our responses.

All action ends in passion. When we are handed over,

Here we glimpse the mystery
of God's incarnation.
God became human
not only to act among us
but also to be the recipient
of our responses.

we wait to be acted upon. This is the mystery of work, the mystery of love, the mystery of friendship, the mystery of community—they always involve being acted upon. And that is the mystery of Jesus' love. Jesus in his passion is the one who waits for our response. Precisely in that waiting the intensity of his love and God's love is revealed to us. If we were forced to love Jesus and to respond to him only as he ordered, we would not really be lovers.

All these insights into Jesus' passion were very important in the discussions with my friend. He realized that after much hard work he had to wait. He came to see that his vocation as a human being would be fulfilled not just in his actions but also in his passion. And together we began to understand that precisely in this waiting some new hope, new peace, and even new joy were gradually emerging. The glory of God was being revealed to us.

The Glory of God and Our Inner Life

Resurrection is not just life after death. First of all, it is the new life that bursts forth in Jesus' passion, in his waiting. The story of Jesus' suffering mysteriously reveals that the resurrection is breaking through even in the midst of the passion. A crowd led by Judas came to Gethsemane. "Then Jesus . . . came forward and said to them, 'Whom do you seek?' They answered him, 'Jesus of Nazareth.' Jesus said to them, 'I am he. . . .' When he said to them, 'I am he,' they drew back and fell to the ground. Again he asked them, 'Whom do you seek?' And they said, 'Jesus of Nazareth.' Jesus answered, 'I told you that I am he; so, if you seek me, let these others go'" (John 18:4–8, RSV).

Precisely when Jesus is being handed over into his passion, he manifests his glory. "Whom do you seek? . . . I am he" are words that echo all the way back to Moses and the burning bush: "I am who I am. I am the one" (see Exod. 3:1–6). These words are the glory of God manifesting itself, and those present fell flat on the ground. Then Jesus was handed over. But already in the handing over we see the glory of God handing himself over to us. God's glory revealed in Jesus embraces passion as well as resurrection.

"The Son of Man," Jesus says, "must be lifted up as

Moses lifted up the serpent in the desert, so that everyone who believes may have eternal life in him" (John 3:14–15, JB). He is lifted up as a passive victim, making the cross a sign of desolation. And he is lifted up in glory, so the cross becomes at the same time a sign of hope. Suddenly we realize that the glory of God, the divinity of God, is bursting through in Jesus' passion precisely when he is most victimized. So new life becomes visible not only in the resurrection on the third day, but already in the passion, in the being handed over. Why? This is because it is in the passion that the fullness of Jesus' love shines through. It is a waiting love, a love that does not seek control. When we allow ourselves to feel fully how we are being acted upon, we can come in touch with a new life that we were not even aware was there. This was the question my sick friend and I talked about constantly. Could he taste the new life in the midst of his passion? Could he see that in his being acted upon by the hospital staff he was already being prepared for a deeper love? It was a love that had been underneath all the action, but he had not tasted it fully. So together we began to see that in the midst of our suffering and passion, in the midst of our waiting, we already begin to experience the resurrection.

In our world today, how much are we really in control? Isn't our life in large part passion? The many ways in which we are acted upon by people, events, the culture in which we live, and the many other factors beyond our control often leave little room for our own initiatives. This becomes especially clear when we notice how many of us are hurt, handicapped, chronically ill, elderly, or restricted economically.

Increasingly in our society we feel we have less and less influence on the decisions that affect our own existence. Therefore it becomes increasingly important to recognize that the largest part of our existence involves waiting in the sense of being acted upon. The life of Jesus tells us that not to be in control is part of the human condition. His vocation and ours are fulfilled not just in action but also in passion, waiting.

Imagine how important this message is for us and for the people in our world. If it is true that God in Jesus Christ is waiting for our response to divine love, then we can discover a whole new perspective on how to wait

It is in the passion
that the fullness of Jesus' love
shines through.
It is a waiting love,
a love that does not seek control.

in life. We can learn to be obedient people who do not always try to go back to the action but who recognize the fulfillment of our deepest humanity in passion, in waiting. If we can do this, I am convinced that we will come in touch with the power and the glory of God and of our own new life. Our service to others will include our helping them see the glory breaking through—not only where they are active but also where they are being acted upon. And so the spirituality of waiting is not simply our waiting for God. It is also participating in God's own waiting for us and in that way coming to share in the deepest love, which is God's love.

The Path of
Living and Dying

A FEW YEARS AGO I was hit by a car and ended up in the hospital. I was feeling very uncomfortable lying on the gurney, but I didn't have any external injuries to speak of so I thought I would be released to return home. When the doctor finally examined me he was kind but clear, saying, "You might not live long. There is serious internal bleeding. We will try to operate but we may not succeed."

Suddenly everything changed. Death was right there in the room with me. I realized that this might be the moment of my death. I felt shocked, and there were many thoughts going through my mind until I had a further experience. I had never felt anything like it before because in the midst of my confusion and shock I became very calm, very "at rest," and there was a sort of "embrace of God" that reassured me and gently told me, "Don't be afraid. You are safe. I am going to bring you home. You belong to me, and I belong to you."

I was so amazingly at peace that later that night after

Most of the material for the following article was taken from two sources, namely, a presentation to the Eighth National Catholic HIV/AIDS conference in Chicago in July 1995, and an interview given to *Crosspoint* magazine (Fall 1995).

"Don't be afraid. You are safe.
I am going to bring you home.
You belong to me,
and I belong to you."

the surgery when I woke up in the intensive care unit, I felt extremely disappointed. I asked myself, "What am I doing here and why am I still alive?" I kept wondering what had happened to me. Gradually I realized that perhaps for the first time in my life I had contemplated my death not through the eyes of fear but through the eyes of love. Somehow, if only for a moment, I had known God, felt unconditionally loved, and I had experienced being a lover.

During my recovery and pondering the whole experience I became aware of some of my life's unfinished business. I was holding on to some particular hurts from the past. I hadn't forgiven certain people, nor had I asked of those I had wounded to be forgiven. I knew that I had also been living apart from the human reality of my death, as though death was far away from me personally. These reflections touched me deeply and I felt that I had been given a gift of extended time to live my life more fully and to better prepare myself for my death. I was deeply convinced in my heart that what I had experienced changed forever how I would live in the world.

Now I am sixty-three years old. I'm aging and I am becoming an elderly person. It is strange to experience myself moving toward old age, and to see others responding to me that way! I may live only another twenty years, another ten years, or another five years. However many years it is, it is only a short time. At my age, the next twenty years will go quickly. Many of my classmates and many members of my family have already died, and these deaths call me to reflect on my own mortality. Because of my "accident experience" and because I am growing older, I am more consistently aware of the wonder, the beauty, and the extreme limitations of my life. I feel inspired to grapple with the reality of my own death in particular and with the great mystery of my life in front of that impending event.

Because so few people talk about it, I begin by asking, "Is death an issue at all?" I realize that for most people in my circles of friends, it is not. The people I know are not entertaining thoughts about death or the fruitfulness of life after their death. My friends say things like, "I see my life becoming less and less productive, but I do hope to live longer," or "I don't want to become a burden to those around me." For some, the thought of having to be cared for by others is almost more than they can bear. This is a big worry for many ill and aging people.

Also, very few people seem to regard death as a *good* thing. That thought is not part of our culture, nor is it visibly part of the church's teachings. When the church speaks about death, it is often about the hereafter, about heaven or hell, or about everlasting life. That is crucial, of course, but it does mean that when we think about death, we think most often about *where* we are going, where we will finally end up, what there is, if anything, to look forward to.

Death through the Eyes of Jesus

What I appreciate as I read Scripture is that Jesus saw death, and his own death in particular, as *more* than a way of getting from one place to another. He saw his death as potentially fruitful in itself, and of enormous benefit to his disciples. Death was not an ending for him but a passage to something much greater.

When Jesus was anticipating his own death he kept repeating the same theme to his disciples: "My death is good for you, because my death will bear many fruits beyond my death. When I die I will not leave you alone, but I will send you my Spirit, the Paraclete, the Counselor. And my Spirit will reveal to you who I am and what I am teaching you. My Spirit will lead you into the truth and will allow you to have a relationship with me that was not possible before my death. My Spirit will help you to form community and grow in strength." Jesus sees that the real fruits of his life will mature *after* his death. That is why he adds, "It is good for you that I go."

If that is true, then the real question for me as I consider my own death is not: how much can I still accomplish before I die, or will I be a burden to others? No, the real question is: how can I live so that my death will be fruitful for others? In other words, how can my death be a gift for my loved ones so that they can reap the fruits of my life after I have died? This question can be answered only if I am first willing to admit Jesus' vision of death as a valid possibility for me.

The real question is:
how can I live so that my death
will be fruitful for others?

Who Was Jesus?

There was that voice, that incredible voice: "You are my beloved son and on you my favor rests." That's the voice at the Jordan River, where Jesus heard and believed that he was the beloved of God on whom God's favor rests. It was as the beloved that Jesus lived his life even in front of the demon. The evil spirit said to him, "Prove that you are the beloved by changing stones into bread and becoming relevant. Prove that you are the beloved by being spectacular and throwing yourself down from the Temple to be saved by God's angels. You'll be in the news and on TV so everyone can see how wonderful you are! Prove that you are the beloved by having power and influence so you can control the situation." But Jesus answered, "I don't have to prove anything. I *am* the beloved because that's the voice I heard in the Jordan River. I know that I am the beloved. I have heard the words, 'You are my beloved. You are my beloved.'" Jesus believed the words and he knew who he was. He lived his whole life as the beloved of God. His spirit was imbued with Love. And Jesus died well because he knew he was going to God and he would soon send his Spirit of Love to his friends. "It is good for you that I leave," he said, "because unless I leave, I cannot send my Spirit who will lead you to the full communion, to the full truth, to the full betrothal." With that Holy Spirit he knew that his beloved apostles would live better, happier lives.

Who Are You?

This vision is not just about Jesus. It is also about you and me. Jesus came to share his identity with you and to tell you that you are the beloved sons and daughters of God. Just for a moment try to enter this enormous mystery, that you, like Jesus, are the beloved daughter or the beloved son of God. This is the truth. Furthermore, your belovedness preceded your birth. You were the beloved before your father, mother, brother, sister, or church loved you or hurt you. You are the beloved because you belong to God from all eternity.

God loved you before you were born, and God will love you after you die. In Scripture God says, "I have loved you with an everlasting love." This is a very fundamental truth of your identity. This is who you are whether you feel it or not. You belong to God from eternity to eternity. Life is just a little opportunity for you during a few years to say, "I love you, too."

If you dare to believe that you are beloved before you are born, you may suddenly realize that your life is very, very special. You become conscious that you were sent here just for a short time, for twenty, forty, or eighty years, to discover and believe that you are a beloved child of God. The length of time doesn't matter. You are sent into this world to believe in yourself as God's chosen one and then to help your brothers and sisters know that they also are beloved sons and daughters of God who belong together. You're sent into this world to be a people of reconciliation. You are sent to heal, to break down the walls between you and your neighbors, locally, nationally, and globally. Before all the distinctions, the separations, and the walls built on foundations of fear, there was unity in the mind and heart of God. Out of that unity, you are sent into this world for a little while to claim that you and every other human being belongs to that same God of Love who lives from eternity to eternity.

If the Love of God blesses you,
you have eyes to see
the blessedness of others.

In this world when you are chosen, you know that somebody else is not chosen. When you are the best, you know that somebody is not the best. When you win and receive a prize, you know there is somebody who lost. But this is not so in the heart of God. If you are chosen in the heart of God, you have eyes to see the chosenness of others. If the Love of God blesses you, you have eyes to see the blessedness of others. The mystery of God's wonderful love is that you come with it into the world and it blesses you whether you know it or not. Your life is in God's universal embrace of the whole human family. So if you look with eyes of faith you discover that you belong to a sacred family. You are son or daughter. You are brother or sister. You are father or mother in the most deeply spiritual way. This little life brings it all together.

Where Are You Going?

Think about the story of Jesus on Mount Tabor. Here is Moses, the leader of the exodus, and here is Elijah, the reminder of the exodus, both long dead, talking with Jesus about his personal departure from this world, his exodus. And with him, mainly listening, are his living apostles, Peter, James, and John. And here is Jesus himself, speaking about his death. This story is like the story of the Red Sea because it is about a journey, a passage, an exodus, a baptism. "I have to undergo a baptism and death is the path," Jesus said. "If you follow me it will be your path too."

One of the most radical demands for you and me is the discovery of our lives as a series of movements or passages. When we are born, we leave our mother's womb for the larger, brighter world of the family. It changes everything, and there is no going back. When we go to school, we leave our homes and families and move to a larger community of people where our lives are forever larger and more expansive. Later when our children are grown and they leave us for more space and freedom than we can offer, our lives may seem less meaningful. It all keeps changing. When we grow older, we retire or lose our jobs, and everything shifts again. It seems as though we are always passing from one phase to the next, gaining and losing someone, some place, something.

You live all these passages in an environment where

One of the most radical demands
for you and me
is the discovery of our lives
as a series of movements
or passages.

you are constantly tempted to be destroyed by resentment, by anger, and by a feeling of being put down. The losses remind you constantly that all isn't perfect and it doesn't always happen for you the way you expected; that perhaps you had hoped events would not have been so painful, but they were; or that you expected something from certain relationships that never materialized. You find yourself disillusioned with the irrevocable personal losses: your health, your lover, your job, your hope, your dream. Your whole life is filled with losses, endless losses. And every time there are losses there are choices to be made. You choose to live your losses as passages to anger, blame, hatred, depression, and resentment, or you choose to let these losses be passages to something new, something wider, and deeper. The question is not how to avoid loss and make it not happen, but how to choose it as a passage, as an exodus to greater life and freedom.

On Mount Tabor Jesus speaks about preparing himself for his final passage. He is not alone, but he is with Moses and Elijah, and with John, Peter, and James. As soon as he comes down from the mountain, Jesus starts talking about how the Son of Man has to suffer and die. The apostles say, "No, no, that's not going to happen to you." But he reminds them that seeing him on the mountaintop full of life is not the whole story. They will also see him in his Passion and on the cross, stripped of life. He invites them to know of his final passage, believing they will finally grasp the amazing mystery of it all. He trusts that it will catapult them into a whole new vision of life and death that cannot be controlled, only lived. Even though they can scarcely grasp it, he assures them with the words, "Don't be afraid."

And after his crucifixion the apostles, filled with the Spirit that Jesus sent to them, survived the loss of Jesus, and their lives gradually moved outward and onward. They fearlessly stood up and announced good news to all the surrounding country because they knew who they were and where they were ultimately going. They found new freedom as disciples and apostles of Jesus, and they were unafraid of persecution and death.

And how does their story touch ours? Where are we going? After a very short visit to earth the time comes for each of us to pass from this world to the next. We have been sent into the world as God's beloved children, and in our passages and our losses we learn to love each other as spouse, parent, brother, or sister. We support one another through the passages of life, and together we grow in love. Finally we ourselves are called to exodus, and we leave the world for full communion with God. It is possible for us, like Jesus, to send our spirit of love to our friends when we leave them. Our spirit, the love we leave behind, is deeply in God's Spirit. It is our greatest gift to those we love.

We, like Jesus, are on a journey, living to make our lives abundantly fruitful through our leaving. When we leave, we will say the words that Jesus said: "It is good for you that I leave, because unless I pass away, I cannot send you my spirit to help you and inspire you."

What Is Fruitfulness in This Context?

Relationships are a mystery. It is possible to have intimate relationships with loved ones who have died. Death sometimes deepens the intimacy. Let me illustrate. You, your father, and your mother are sharing around the

139

We, like Jesus,
are on a journey,
living to make our lives
abundantly fruitful
through our leaving.

kitchen table. It is probably quite ordinary, and you talk about the events of the day or the weather. But if you leave home for a while and travel to a foreign country, and you write your mother and father, you'll sometimes say things in your letters that were never said around the table. You might say, "Mom, I really love you. Dad, I think of you and I miss you a lot, and I wish you were here." These are the kinds of intimate expressions that you don't use when you are together. It is interesting that a little absence, a little distance, may allow you to experience intimacy in a relationship that you were not able to feel when you were physically together.

Of course, dying is a much more radical leaving than taking a trip. I do believe though that after separation certain people continue to be very significant for us in our hearts and through our memories. Remembering them is much more than just thinking of them, because we are making them part of our members, part of our whole being.

Knowing this experience allows me to live from the deep belief that I have love to offer to people, not only here, but also beyond my short, little life. I am a human being who was loved by God before I was born and whom God will love after I die. This brief lifetime is my opportunity to receive love, deepen love, grow in love, and give love. When I die love continues to be active, and from full communion with God I am present by love to those I leave behind.

We are living in a culture that measures the value of the human person by degrees of success and productivity. What is your title? How much money do you make? How many friends do you have? What are your accomplishments? How busy are you? What do your children do? But it is important for us to remember that as we grow older our ability to succeed in this way gradually diminishes. We lose our titles, our friends, our accomplishments, and our ability to do many things, because we begin to feel weaker, more vulnerable, and more dependent. If we continue to look at ourselves from the point of view of success, our condition is not a good one! Because of our strong cultural vision, it is a huge challenge to look at vulnerability not as a negative thing but as a positive thing. Do we dare to look at weakness as an opportunity to become fruitful? Fruitfulness in the

This brief lifetime
is my opportunity to receive love,
deepen love, grow in love,
and give love.

spiritual life is about love, and this fruitfulness is very different from success or productivity.

It is interesting to remember that fruits are always the result of vulnerability. A child is conceived when two people are vulnerable to each other in their intimacy. The experience of peace and reconciliation comes when people are very honest and compassionate with one another, when they are vulnerable and open about their mistakes and weaknesses. The seed that falls into broken ground bears much fruit. So perhaps it is wise to begin to shift our thinking. We want to move away from emulating successfulness and begin to dream about a life of fruitfulness.

When he was dying on the cross, Jesus was ultimately vulnerable. He had nothing left. Everything had been taken from him, including his dignity, and in the eyes of his culture he was a failure. But in all truth the moment of his death on the cross was his life's greatest moment, because there his life became the most fruitful one in all history. Jesus saw his life and his death as fruitful. "It is good for you that I go. I will send you my Spirit."

Our weakness and old age call people to surround

*By not resisting weakness
and by gratefully receiving
another's care
we call forth community.*

us and support us. By not resisting weakness and by gratefully receiving another's care we call forth community and provide our caregivers an opportunity to give their own gifts of compassion, care, love, and service. As we are given into their hands, others are blessed and enriched by caring for us. Our weakness bears fruit in their lives.

And dying is our ultimate vulnerability. Instead of looking at the weakness of old age as simply the experience of loss after loss, we can choose it as a passage to emptiness where our hearts have room to be filled with the Spirit of Love overflowing. It is ultimate weakness, but it is also potentially the greatest moment of our fruitfulness.

Fear of Death

Fear in the face of death is natural because death is a mystery. The fear of death resides in me, but I want to approach my death with fear being less dominant. Scripture says that the opposite of fear is love. "Perfect love casts out fear." Believing this Word I grapple with fear and direct my life's energies toward loving God, others, and myself more deeply. The truth is that, like Jesus, most of us choose to give our lives and our deaths for others. We try to live so that others may be blessed by our lives and our deaths. We trust that life and death are not about fate or destiny. We then say with Jesus, "It is good for you that I go." This way of living minimizes the fear of dying.

I have many friends who have died beautifully. They said: "I'm going to die. I've had a beautiful life, and I'm grateful. I give myself over to God, and I want you to remember me." When someone I love dies that way, I can really grieve and celebrate because the memory of my friend is such a gift of grace to me.

I must add that I do believe that what I am saying here is almost impossible to do alone. We need friends around us who believe that this is true. In my community four people died in the last few years. Helen was ill for a long time, but there was someone with her day and night and she was not alone when she died. Lloyd died rather unexpectedly, but we had a few days during which we surrounded him. When he died there was a lot of grief and pain, mingled with the strength that comes from being with one another through it all. As this dear brother called us around him in death we reminded him: "We are with you. Don't be afraid. God is calling you home, but you will always be part of our ongoing life."

So the fear of death is not something we handle well on our own. We need other people around us whispering in our ears, "Don't be afraid to die, because even when you die, you will stay with us in a very deep way."

Learning to Remember the Dead

Before he died, Jesus said to his disciples, "Stay together, pray and wait for the Spirit to come." They didn't really understand what he was saying, and besides, because of his death, they were in deep grief. They needed to question what had happened and who was to blame. They needed time to cry, to go over past events, and to miss their friend and leader, Jesus. They needed to feel his absence and to want desperately to have him back. Only after time and when they finally could say, "Yes he's really gone," could they receive his presence in another way.

"Don't be afraid to die,
because even when you die,
you will stay with us
in a very deep way."

So too for us when someone we love dies. It belongs to the call of all Christians to let people really die, not just in the sense of burying them, but to let die our experience of their physical presence, to let them die *within* us. That journey through grief may take years! We expect her or look for her. We want him back. We search for the meaning in her death. With the passing of a full year Christmas comes and he is absent. Easter comes and we know she won't be here. His birthday, our wedding anniversary, and with the arrival of every other important date of the year we feel afresh the incredible absence.

We gradually accept that she is not on another trip or on her vacation. We hear or read something we want to share with him, and then we suddenly remember that he is not coming back. She is gone for good, always, absolutely gone. After a time we may begin to feel that we have done the work of grieving when unexpectedly something reminds us again of our loss, and we are suddenly plunged into sadness all over again. That is because the person we have loved is *in* us, part of our soul, part of our interior life, and the letting go is enormously painful.

This is why it takes a long time to let someone we love die completely.

Ever so slowly as these events pass one by one, we begin to know and accept that the relationship, as we knew it, is irrevocably gone. And as we allow the dead to be gone from our lives, they gently begin to take on another, new life within us and within our memories. We still miss them, but we somehow choose life without them physically present to us, and we revive with a new vision, new energy, and new strength.

I witnessed this transformation in my own father when my mother died in 1978. He mourned her loss deeply. They were companions, and they had lived together for many, many years. Her death changed everything for my father, and he had to adapt to a whole new life without her. But with time he eventually began to live something new, holding her memory, but not clinging to it in a false way. He was able to acknowledge that he had a beautiful life and a beautiful family with her, but he had to let her go. And as he did that there seemed to be a new joy in him, a new freedom, a new maturity.

I have also known people who could not seem to let

As we allow the dead
to be gone from our lives,
they gently begin to take on
another, new life within us
and within our memories.

go of their grief. They may have felt unfaithful or guilty to find new life as a widow or a widower. This is false piety. Death, our own or that of loved ones, is not our worst enemy. Jesus came to show us about life and death, and Jesus speaks of his death not as a failure but as an opportunity to send his Spirit. If we keep our eyes on Jesus and if we carefully read the Gospels, we begin to see that new life is sent to us after the death of a loved one. It does not mean, of course, that death is wonderful and there is no grief or pain. Death, in itself, is not wonderful. It is terrible. But how we see our death and the death of others we know and love can be transforming. It takes time. But it is possible.

My mother died, many of my classmates died, and a number of very close friends died in recent years. I remember each of them, not in a morbid way but as having finally reached their true home. Meanwhile, I am still on the way home. Those who have died live on in me and inspire me with their example and the rich legacy of love from their earthly lives. Their lives touch mine. Their lives make a difference in mine. Unfortunately there isn't much recognition of the spiritual significance of a loved one's death because our culture would have us deal with our grief by going on as though nothing significant had happened.

Love transforms our death or another's from nightmare to gift. As part of a family or community we make the dead part of our members so as to receive the gift of their spirits. Loved ones who have died are remembered in worship and prayers, in conversations, with photographs, and by visiting their graves. Life does go on, but with their remembrance enriching our hearts.

Befriending Death

Intuitively I feel that when someone is dying young, in their twenties or thirties, their span of life has been too brief to grasp how special they are and how fruitful their short life is. I sometimes witness this with friends suffering from AIDS who are suddenly brought face to face with the mystery of the radical finality of death. They are easily overwhelmed with grief and anger. I feel deeply for them, and I also grieve because they do not comprehend or appreciate their abundant fruitfulness. I realize that these youthful brothers and sisters have a great challenge to befriend death.

Because I have lived many years there is, for me, an option about preparing to die. I know that I have no choice about how long I will live, but I do have a decision about *how* to live, and a choice about how I will face my aging, and about how I will live my exodus. I may be bedridden and that will be totally out of my control, but with my faculties I choose now the way I will live my declining years.

After my accident a few years ago and after my experience of peace with regard to my death, I felt very open and free to welcome and spend time with those who came to visit. One of the most startling things for me about those visits was the number of people who said to me, "Henri, you are a much better pastor when you are sick than when you are healthy! Finally you are taking time to listen. You're not so preoccupied. You're not hurrying crazily from one thing to another and you are much more lighthearted! What you say now is so helpful. We really enjoy the visits!"

At sixty-three I am very aware that for me it is just

a question of years, a few years. And so I sense that my aging is a time for me to be thinking of my passage to more abundant life. I want to become grateful that my life will come to completion and to anticipate sending my spirit of love to all those I cherish. I feel the need to talk about my death not morbidly, but openly, and to invite my community, my family, and my friends to be with me on the path to the end of my earthly life. I want to befriend my death.

Conclusion

God is Spirit and the Source of all love. Our spiritual journey calls us to seek and find this living God of Love in prayer, worship, spiritual reading, spiritual mentoring, compassionate service to the poor, and good friends. Let us claim the truth that we are loved and open our hearts to receive God's overflowing love poured out for us. And living fully each day let us share that love in all our wonderful and difficult relationships, responsibilities, and passages.

The seeds of death are at work in us, but love is

stronger than death. Your death and mine is our final passage, our exodus to the full realization of our identity as God's beloved children and to full communion with the God of love. Jesus walked the path ahead of us and invites us to choose the same path during our lifetime. He calls to us, "Follow Me." He assures us. "Do not be afraid." This is our faith.

Henri Nouwen Literary Centre
11339 Yonge Street
Richmond Hill, Ontario L4S 1L1
nouwencentre@nouwen.net
www.nouwen.net